DEAD MAN'S ISLAND

When someone has a secret and doesn't want other people to know about it, we say that they have 'a skeleton in the cupboard'. Most people have secrets they are not proud of. Carol Sanders has. She has a 'skeleton', and it follows her wherever she goes. Her secret makes her more and more unhappy; slowly, but certainly, it is ruining her life.

And then Carol meets someone with an even bigger secret. His secret is so big that he needs a whole island to hide it on. Perhaps Carol is the best person to find out what his secret is. But if she does, what will he do? Will he be pleased to share his secret, or will he be angry, very angry? It depends what his secret is. It all depends what kind of 'skeleton' he is hiding behind the locked door – the locked door that Carol is going to open.

OXFORD BOOKWORMS LIBRARY

Thriller & Adventure

Dead Man's Island

Stage 2 (700 headwords)

Series Editor: Jennifer Bassett
Founder Editor: Tricia Hedge
Activities Editors: Jennifer Bassett and Alison Baxter

JOHN ESCOTT

Dead Man's Island

OXFORD UNIVERSITY PRESS

OXFORD
UNIVERSITY PRESS

Great Clarendon Street, Oxford OX2 6DP

Oxford University Press is a department of the University of Oxford.
It furthers the University's objective of excellence in research, scholarship,
and education by publishing worldwide in

Oxford New York

Auckland Cape Town Dar es Salaam Hong Kong Karachi
Kuala Lumpur Madrid Melbourne Mexico City Nairobi
New Delhi Shanghai Taipei Toronto

With offices in

Argentina Austria Brazil Chile Czech Republic France Greece
Guatemala Hungary Italy Japan Poland Portugal Singapore
South Korea Switzerland Thailand Turkey Ukraine Vietnam

OXFORD and OXFORD ENGLISH are registered trade marks of
Oxford University Press in the UK and in certain other countries

ISBN 978 0 19 479055 0

A complete recording of this Bookworms edition of
Dead Man's Island is available in a CD pack ISBN 978 0 19 478978 3

Printed in China

Illustrated by: Alan Marks

Word count (main text): 5215 words

For more information on the Oxford Bookworms Library,
visit www.oup.com/elt/gradedreaders

CONTENTS

Coming to England

My name is Carol Sanders.

I live in England now, but when I was younger, I lived in Hong Kong. My father was a businessman there and my mother worked as a secretary. We lived in Hong Kong for seven years.

I was happy at school, with lots of friends, and we had a good time. I liked pop music – the Rolling Stones, David Bowie and Jake Rosso were my favourites.

Jake Rosso was my favourite singer. He died in a car accident the year I left school, but I listened to his pop records all the time. I had hundreds of pictures and photos of him on my bedroom wall.

Then one day in winter when I was seventeen, things began to go wrong for me.

My father went to Australia on business. I loved him very much and didn't like him going away.

'Come home quickly,' I always said to him.

He was in Australia for two weeks. Then, on the day of his journey home, an aeroplane from Sydney crashed into the sea just south of Hong Kong. Everybody on the plane died.

I heard about the plane crash on television. At first, I did not think about my father. Then I remembered he was flying back from Sydney on that day.

'Oh, no!' I cried.

I telephoned the airport but they did not know the names of all the passengers then.

'Perhaps my father didn't get that plane,' I thought. 'Oh, please! Please!'

My mother was at work and I called her on the telephone. She came home quickly and we went to the airport and waited for news.

Later, we learned my father was on the plane.

'It's not true!' I shouted.

But it was true, and I began to cry.

I was happy in Hong Kong.

I cried for weeks and weeks. I spent many days alone in my room. I was lonely and sad and I wanted to die, too.

I stopped going out with my friends. I didn't want to see other people. I stopped listening to Jake Rosso's records, and took his pictures off my bedroom wall. I didn't listen to music or watch television. Nothing mattered any more.

Then I stopped crying. I stopped feeling sad and began to feel angry.

'Why did it happen to him?' I asked my mother. 'Why do the best people die? Jake Rosso. My father.'

'I . . . I don't know, Carol,' my mother said. She was unhappy, too.

At the time of the plane crash, I was a student at college. I enjoyed the work and college life very much, but after my father's death I stopped doing my work at the college. I began to go out with some new friends. They were different from my other friends, and my mother didn't like them.

'They're bad people, Carol,' she told me. 'They do dangerous things.'

'They're exciting,' I said. 'And I like them.'

I knew she was angry but I didn't care. But then I learned my new friends took drugs, and I began to take drugs, too. It was wrong and stupid, I know that now, but I was unhappy and angry.

The police came to the college to arrest some of the

students. They didn't arrest me, but I had to leave the college. It was a bad time.

My mother was very unhappy with me. 'What am I going to do with you, Carol?' she said.

'I'm sorry,' I told her.

'We'll go back to England,' she said. 'You can find a college there. Perhaps you can be happier in England.'

'All right,' I said. 'I want to forget what's happened. I want to forget what I've done and begin a new life, be a new person.'

I knew my mother was angry, but I didn't care.

5

A month later, we came back to England. We lived in London, in a hotel. It was strange, at first, with all the red buses and everybody speaking English. It was the beginning of the summer, three months before college began in the autumn. London was full of tourists.

We looked at all the famous buildings – Buckingham Palace, The Tower of London. And we went to restaurants and theatres in the evenings. It was interesting and exciting and I began to forget the bad times in Hong Kong.

'I'm pleased we came to London,' I told my mother.

But after a few weeks, she said, 'You need to find a college, Carol. You must go on studying. And I need a job.'

That evening, we looked in the newspapers.

'What about this?' I said. I showed my mother a job in the newspaper.

SECRETARY
for the summer months
on a small private island in Scotland.
Live with the family in a big house.
Interesting work and good pay
for the right person.

Phone Greta Ross. Telephone number 071 . . .

*London was interesting and exciting, and I began to forget the
bad times in Hong Kong.*

'Well, that sounds interesting,' said my mother. 'I'd like to work as a secretary on an island in Scotland. It's a beautiful country, Carol, and you can go to a college there in the autumn.'

'And it's a place to live for the summer,' I said. 'Hotels are expensive.'

My mother telephoned Greta Ross.

'Come and see me tomorrow,' Greta Ross told her. 'Come to the Savoy Hotel at eleven o'clock.'

I went to the Savoy Hotel with my mother. It was big and expensive, bigger than our hotel, and in the centre of London.

'Mum needs this job,' I thought. 'And a private island in Scotland is a nice place to live. Perhaps I can forget what's happened if I go there.'

'Room twenty-two,' said the woman at the hotel desk. 'Go on up. Mrs Ross will see you now.'

Greta Ross was waiting for us. She was about thirty years old and very beautiful. She wore an expensive red dress and her hair was very long and dark.

'This is my daughter, Carol,' said my mother.

'Hallo, Carol,' said Greta Ross.

'Hallo,' I said.

'Carol is eighteen years old,' said my mother. 'Can she come with me, if I get the job? Perhaps she can help in the

Greta Ross was waiting for us.

house or in the gardens. She likes gardening. She's studying farming at college.'

'Perhaps,' said Greta Ross. 'There's a small farm on the island.'

'I'd like to work on the farm,' I said.

Greta Ross looked at my mother. 'How long did you live in Hong Kong, Mrs Sanders?'

'Seven years,' answered my mother. 'My husband died in a plane crash last year, so we've come back to live in England.'

'Where did you live before Hong Kong?'

'We lived in India for three years.'

Then Greta Ross took my mother into a room and asked her more questions. I waited outside.

'Greta Ross is nice,' I thought. 'I hope my mother gets the job.'

Soon after, the door opened and my mother came out. She was smiling.

Greta Ross said, 'Please wait here for a minute, Mrs Sanders. I want to make a phone call.' She went back into the room, and closed the door.

I was sitting on a chair near the door, and I could just hear Greta Ross's voice speaking on the phone.

'I think I've found someone,' she was saying. 'She has a daughter, but the girl can work in the garden or on the farm . . . Don't worry, they've been away from England for ten years ... It'll be all right, I tell you ... Don't worry.'

After a few minutes, Greta Ross put down the phone and came out of the room.

'You've got the job,' she told my mother.

My mother was pleased. 'Thank you,' she replied.

I was pleased, too, but now I was worried about that phone call. I didn't understand it.

I could just hear Greta Ross's voice speaking on the phone.

2

The Island

We went to Scotland the next day, first by plane, then by train. Greta Ross travelled with us.

I looked out of the train window and saw fields and villages and mountains. 'Mum is right,' I thought. 'Scotland is a very beautiful place.'

'You're going to be my husband's secretary,' Greta Ross told my mother. 'He's a businessman, but he never leaves the island. He does all his work by telephone and letter and computer. He invests money in companies, all over the world.'

'Do many people live on the island?' I asked.

'Not many,' said Greta Ross. 'You'll meet them soon.'

'Greta Ross is young,' I thought. 'Is her husband young, too? How can a young man buy an island? Is he very rich?'

After the train, we went on Mr Ross's boat, which took us out to the island. The boatman was a young man. He had dark hair and was brown from the sun.

'This is Tony,' said Greta Ross. 'He works for Mr Ross.'

'Hi,' said Tony.

Soon we were near the island. I could see the beaches and the cliffs. The boat slowed down.

'There are dangerous rocks around the island,' explained

12

Tony. 'A lot of them are under the water and you can't see them. I have to be careful. But the rocks keep other boats away, and that pleases Mr Ross.'

'Why?' I asked.

Tony looked at Greta Ross but she wasn't listening. 'Mr Ross doesn't like visitors to the island,' Tony said in a quiet voice.

Then Greta Ross looked at us and Tony said no more.

'Why doesn't Mr Ross like visitors?' I thought. 'Has he something to hide?'

When we arrived on the island, my mother and I followed Greta up to the house. It was very big and there were trees all around it.

A woman was waiting inside the house.

'This is Mrs Duncan, Tony's mother,' said Greta. 'She's the housekeeper and her husband is the gardener. Mrs Duncan will take you up to your rooms. I'm going to tell Mr Ross you've arrived.'

The housekeeper was a little woman with short hair. She went up the stairs, and my mother and I went after her.

My room was next to my mother's. I looked out of the window and saw the gardens at the back of the house. A man was working in the garden, near some trees. 'Is that Mr Duncan?' I thought. I looked between the trees and saw the sea. 'It's a beautiful house and a beautiful island.'

'Mr Ross doesn't like visitors to the island,' Tony said.

That evening, we had dinner with Mr and Mrs Duncan and Tony. We ate in the big kitchen.

'What happened to Mr Ross's last secretary?' asked my mother.

'She's in hospital,' replied Mrs Duncan. 'She's going to be away all summer.'

'Isn't Mrs Ross lonely here?' I said.

'No,' said Mrs Duncan. 'She likes painting a lot. She has a room upstairs and goes there to paint. She's very good. Sometimes she goes to different places on the island to paint pictures.'

We finished eating our meal. Soon after, Greta Ross came into the kitchen.

'Mr Ross wants to see you and your daughter now, Mrs Sanders,' she said. 'Follow me, please.'

We followed her through the house and into a big room. This was Mr Ross's office and he was sitting behind a desk.

I was surprised. He was a young man, about thirty. He had a moustache, short dark hair, and he wore glasses.

Mr Ross was speaking into the telephone. 'Who does he look like?' I thought. 'Is it Tony Duncan?'

'Mr Ross is talking to a business friend in New York,' said Greta. 'Please, sit down.'

While we waited, I looked around the office. There were three telephones, a computer, and lots of books and papers.

'*Who does he look like?*' *I thought.*

There was another door and I could see a smaller room, next to the office. There was a smaller desk and another computer in there.

Mr Ross finished speaking on the phone, then looked carefully at my mother and me. For a few seconds he didn't speak, and just watched us. Then he said, 'I'm pleased to meet you, Mrs Sanders. I need some help with my work. My secretary is in hospital, and there's a lot of work to do. Sometimes you'll have to work late at night, because of time differences in New York and Tokyo. Is that all right?'

'Yes, that's all right,' said my mother.

'Can you use a computer?'

'Yes.'

'Good.' He looked at me. 'Is this your daughter?'

'Yes, this is Carol,' said my mother.

'Hallo,' I said.

'Greta says you like gardening. There's a big garden here, so you can help Mr Duncan. And there's a farm. Dan and Stella Parks live in the farmhouse and work on the farm. You can help them, too. We have some animals. Some sheep, a few cows and chickens. And there's a horse called Smoke. He's grey, like his name. Can you ride?'

'Yes,' I said. 'I can ride a horse.'

'You can ride Smoke around the island, if you like.'

'I'd like that,' I said. 'Thank you.'

'And we grow vegetables and fruit,' he said. 'I work on the farm sometimes. I enjoy it.'

I smiled at him but he didn't smile back.

'Carol will enjoy working on the farm,' said my mother. 'Won't you, Carol?'

'Yes,' I said.

'Mr Ross looks sad,' I thought. 'But how did he get all his money? And why does he hide away on an island?'

3

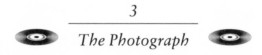 *The Photograph*

I worked in the garden for the first two days. The weather was hot and sunny. I liked working with Mr Duncan, and he was pleased with my work.

'You're a good gardener,' he said.

'I've always liked gardening,' I said. 'But I'm studying at college to be a farmer.'

Sometimes I saw Greta Ross.

'She likes to be alone,' I thought. Once or twice I saw Greta go out with her painting things. She went up on the hills or down to the beach.

Mr Duncan took me to the farm and I met Dan and Stella Parks. They were very friendly.

'You can work on the farm for the next three days,' said

in many companies and countries. But it's not his money.'

'It's not?' I was surprised by this.

'No, it's his wife's money. And she bought the island. It's her island, her house, her farm. Everything belongs to her.'

'How strange. But why does Mr Ross always look sad? And why does he never leave the island?' I asked.

'I don't know,' said my mother. 'He says he likes it here and likes working on his farm. It's strange, I know.'

Sometimes, when I finished work, I walked along the beaches or the cliffs. Or I went swimming in the sea. I liked swimming. Greta Ross often came to the beach to swim, but Mr Ross never came.

'Stay away from the rocks, Carol,' Greta Ross told me. 'They're very dangerous.'

'I will,' I said.

Sometimes I took my camera to the beach and took photographs of some of the boats that went by. I took photographs of the birds on the cliffs.

There were other small islands near our island, and boats with tourists stopped at them. But no boats stopped at our island. They kept away from the dangerous rocks. Tony was right. The island did not have visitors.

One day, I was walking back to the house, and had my camera with me. I stopped and looked at the big house.

Mr Duncan was working in the garden in front of it. At first, he didn't see me.

'I'm going to take a photograph of the house,' I thought. 'The sun is in just the right place, and it will make a good picture.'

I looked at the building through my camera, and took the photograph. Mr Ross was coming out of a door. He was in my picture, too, and he looked angry.

'That's all right,' I thought. 'It's still a good photograph.'

But Mr Duncan was running across the grass. He came quickly up to me and said, 'Give me your camera.' He looked very worried.

'What's wrong?' I asked in surprise. I gave him the camera.

'Never take photographs of Mr Ross,' he said. And then he opened the back of my camera and took out the film.

'Hey! What are you doing?' I said. 'You'll spoil my film!'

But he didn't stop. 'Sorry,' he said, and he put the film into his pocket. 'But no pictures of Mr Ross. He doesn't like people to take pictures of him.'

Mr Ross was watching us. He saw the camera and he saw Mr Duncan take out the film, but he said nothing. Then he turned and went back into the house.

Later, I told my mother about Mr Duncan and the camera. 'He spoiled my film,' I said.

'Hey! What are you doing?' I said. 'You'll spoil my film!'

'I don't understand,' she said. 'Why did he do that?'

'I don't know,' I said, 'but there's something strange about Mr Ross.'

About a week later, I finished work early one day and came back to the house. My mother was working in her small room, next to Mr Ross's office. Mrs Duncan was in the kitchen. Greta Ross was painting in her room upstairs.

I went to my room and began reading a book. I was sitting beside the window. After half an hour, I got tired of reading. I looked out at the rain, and the grey sea and rocks between the trees.

'My book isn't very interesting,' I thought.

I got up and went out of my room. I walked along the passage and turned a corner. Then I saw the door at the end of the passage. There was a large plant in a plant pot outside the door.

'Where does that door go?' I thought. 'I haven't seen it before.' I remembered the face at the window in my first week on the island. 'Perhaps it's the door to *that* room,' I thought.

I walked along to the door and turned the handle. The door didn't move. It was locked.

'What are you doing!' said a voice behind me.

I turned round quickly and saw Greta Ross. She looked angry.

Greta Ross looked angry. 'That room is private,' she said.

'That room is private,' she said.
'I'm sorry,' I said. 'I didn't—'
'Stay away from there,' she told me.

* * *

25

I told my mother about the locked door.

'What's behind it?' I said. 'Is it a secret?'

'I don't know,' said my mother. 'It doesn't matter. Mr Ross can have locked rooms if he wants them.'

'I think he does have secrets,' I said. 'There's something strange about him. There's something strange about this island. Somebody isn't telling us something. Something important.'

My mother laughed. 'Stop playing detective, Carol,' she said.

4

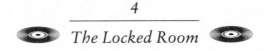 *The Locked Room*

T wo days later there was a storm in the middle of the night.

I was hot and I couldn't sleep. I got out of bed, went across to the window and looked out at the night. Black clouds hurried across the sky, and the trees moved wildly in the wind. The rain made a loud noise on the window.

I opened my window and put my head out into the wind and the rain. I looked at the other windows in the house. Most of them were dark. But one window had a light in it. 'Somebody isn't sleeping,' I thought. 'Which room is that?'

There were six windows between my window and the room with the light.

'And there are six doors between my room and the locked door!' I thought. 'That light is in the locked room. Somebody's in there!'

I put on my dressing-gown and went out of my room. The house was dark, and at first I couldn't see very well. I walked along the passage and turned the corner.

There it was, the locked room. And there was a light under the door!

I went nearer and heard noises.

'Somebody's moving about in the locked room,' I thought. 'Who is it?'

Then the light went off and the door opened.

I was afraid to move.

Somebody came out of the room, and into the dark passage. Lightning suddenly lit up the house, and I saw who it was.

'It's Mr Ross!' I thought. 'What was he doing in that room in the middle of the night?'

I didn't move and he didn't see me. He locked the door of the room carefully. He didn't put the key in his pocket, but hid it in the plant pot next to the door.

'He's coming along here,' I thought. 'I must get back to my room.'

And I ran back along the passage.

Mr Ross hid the key in the plant pot next to the door.

Mr Ross heard me. 'Who's that?' he called.

I didn't answer, but ran into my room and closed the door.

He came along the passage and stopped outside my door. Then he walked past and went on down the stairs.

I took off my dressing-gown and went back to bed. I was shaking because I was afraid.

'Now I know how to get into the locked room,' I thought. 'But what's in there?'

There was no storm in the morning, but it was still raining. I got up early and worked on the farm. There were eggs from the chickens and I put them in boxes. I helped to milk the cows and then took them out to the field.

Later, I went back into the house for breakfast. 'Did you sleep all right last night?' asked Mrs Duncan. 'Or did the storm wake you up?'

'I . . . slept all right,' I said. I didn't want to tell her about the light in the locked room, or about Mr Ross.

After breakfast, I went back upstairs. Mr Ross was talking on the telephone in his office. My mother was working at her desk. I knew that Mrs Duncan was in the kitchen and that Mr Duncan was working in the garden.

'Where's Mrs Ross?' I thought.

Then I looked out of the window and saw her with Tony Duncan. They were walking to the boat.

'He's taking her out in the boat,' I thought. 'Perhaps she's going to Edinburgh.'

The boat moved away from the island and I waited until it was out at sea. Then I opened the door of my room.

There was nobody in the passage and I ran along to the locked room. The key was still in the plant pot and I took it out. My hand was shaking.

Then I unlocked the door.

5

A Dead Man

I went into the room . . . and I was very surprised.
The room was full of strange things. Coloured shirts
and suits. Three guitars. And there were posters and
photographs on the walls.

I looked at the posters.

Jake Rosso's face looked down at me.

I looked at the dead Jake Rosso's picture, and I
remembered all the photographs on the walls of my room
in Hong Kong. I could never forget that face – the face of
my favourite singer.

Then, while I looked at his face, something strange happened. I began to see another face in the posters. An older face, and with a moustache, but the *same* face.

I saw the face of Mr Ross.

'No!' I said. 'It's not true!'

But it was, I knew it was.

'Mr Ross is . . . *Jake Rosso!*'

I looked at the dead Jake Rosso's picture – and I saw the face of Mr Ross!

31

'No!' said a voice behind me.

I turned round and saw Mr Ross. He was standing in the doorway. He looked . . . afraid.

'I don't believe you!' I said.

'You have to believe me!'

I looked at the posters. 'Who is that, if it's not you?'

'It's Jake Rosso. He was . . . my brother.'

'That's not true!' I shouted. 'I don't believe you. Listen, Jake Rosso was my favourite singer – I had hundreds of photos of him. I still have all his records. I *loved* him, do you understand? Thousands of people loved him.'

'He's dead,' Mr Ross said quietly.

'*No!*' I shouted. 'You're Jake Rosso! You look different now, yes. You've got short hair, you've got a moustache now, and you wear glasses. But you're . . . Jake . . . Rosso. You were my favourite pop star, so I *know.*'

Mr Ross said nothing, and watched my face.

'He doesn't know what to do,' I thought. 'He knows I don't believe him, and he's afraid.'

Then he said, 'It was you in the passage last night, wasn't it?'

'Yes,' I answered.

He looked angry. 'I was wrong to give your mother a job,' he said. 'I thought it was OK because you came from Hong Kong. And I needed help with my work. I needed a good secretary.'

'You're Jake Rosso!' I shouted.

'Does your other secretary know who you are?' I asked. 'Do the other people on the island know?'

Mr Ross didn't answer, but walked across to the window. He was thinking.

'What's he going to do?' I thought.

Then he turned round. 'OK, you're right. I . . . I am Jake Rosso.'

'I *knew* it!'

He looked worried and unhappy. 'Can you keep a secret? A very important secret?'

I thought for a minute, then I said, 'Yes, I can keep a secret.'

Then he told me.

'The other people on this island are my family.'

'Your family?' I said.

'Yes. My real name is James Duncan, and Mr and Mrs Duncan are my father and mother. Tony is my younger brother, and his wife, Lisa, is my secretary. It's she who's in hospital.'

'And Dan and Stella Parks?' I asked.

'My mother's sister and her husband,' he said.

'But what are you doing here on this island? I don't understand.'

'I'll tell you,' he said. He sat down on a chair and took a guitar in his hands, but he didn't play it. 'You were right. I was a famous pop star. I was very rich, and I had a beautiful wife. But things went wrong.'

'How?'

'I took drugs,' he said. 'I drank a lot of alcohol. I got drunk and crashed cars. I did stupid, terrible things. I knew it was wrong but I couldn't stop doing it. I was . . . crazy, for a time.'

'I can understand that,' I told him. 'I've taken drugs, too.'

He looked surprised. 'You have?'

'Yes,' I said. 'After my father died, I was very unhappy and things went wrong for me too. But go on with your story.'

He went on. 'One night, I was driving my car. I was drunk and – and I hit somebody. A young girl. She . . . died. I killed her.'

'Oh, no!'

'Yes,' he said. 'She was fifteen years old. I wanted to die, too. The money didn't matter any more. Nothing mattered any more.'

'What did you do after the accident?' I asked.

'I drove on in the car. I didn't stop, and I didn't tell the police. I had killed someone and I was afraid.' He looked afraid now. He put the guitar down and went on with his story. 'So I made a plan. Jake Rosso had to die, too. It was the best thing to do. And so . . . I "killed" him.'

'But you're still alive.'

'My family know I'm alive, but no other people know.' He looked at me. 'But now *you* know.'

'How did you do it?' I asked.

'I told my family about my plan and I told Greta, my

'I hit a young girl, and she died. I killed her.'

wife. At first they didn't like it. But after a long time, they said OK. Then I faked the car crash.'

'*Faked* it?'

'Yes,' he said. 'I put some of my things in the car. A guitar, and some clothes. Then I pushed my car over a cliff and burned it. The police found the burned car and thought I was dead. Everybody thought I was killed in the car crash.'

'But you faked the crash,' I said.

'Yes.'

'What did you do then?'

'My family hid me away for months. I tried to change into a different person – shorter hair, a moustache, quiet suits. All my money went to Greta and she changed her name to Ross. I told her to buy this island. Now I invest her money, the money that was mine. And now I'm "James Ross".'

'What about "Jake Rosso"?' I asked.

'Jake Rosso took drugs,' he said. 'Jake Rosso got drunk and crashed cars. He killed a young girl, so he had to "die". I can never forget the girl. I think about her every day.'

'And that's why you always look so sad,' I thought.

I looked around the room. 'Why do you keep a room like this? Why do you keep the guitars, the posters and photographs?'

'Everybody thought I was killed in the car crash.'

James Ross did not speak for a minute. Then he said, 'I need to remember my old life, and what Jake Rosso was like. I'm never going to sing again and I'm never going to take drugs. But I need this room, to remember.'

I looked at the posters and the photographs. And I looked at his sad face. 'I'm not going to say anything. I won't tell my mother, I won't tell anybody.'

James Ross looked at me. 'I think you understand,' he said.

'I do,' I said. 'I've done bad things. I want to forget them, too. I needed to get away, to hide, too. That's why we came to England, to begin a new life. Yes, I understand.'

He took my hand, and we walked out of the room and closed the door.

I never went into the room again, and I didn't tell anybody.

My mother and I left the island at the end of the summer. Soon after, I went to college.

My life is better now. I work on a farm in England and my mother works in an office. My mother doesn't worry about me, because I'm happier now.

I haven't been back to the island.

But I know there's a 'dead man' living there.

I haven't been back to the island. But I know there's a 'dead man' living there.

GLOSSARY

alcohol drinks like beer, wine, whisky, etc.

arrest when the police catch someone and take them to prison

care (didn't care) to feel that something is (not) interesting or (not) important

cliff the high, steep side of a hill

college a place where people go to study after they leave school

company a number of people who work together in business

crazy mad; very stupid

dressing-gown a warm coat to put over night clothes

drugs dangerous things that people eat or smoke or put into their bodies

drunk *(adj)* when somebody cannot walk or talk clearly after drinking too much alcohol

fake *(v)* to make or do something that looks real but is not real

farm a place where you grow food and keep animals

glasses round pieces of glass that you wear over the eyes to see better

handle *(n)* the part of a door that you hold to open it

housekeeper a person who looks after a house

invest to put money into a business and get more money back later

lightning a sudden very bright light in the sky during a storm

moustache the hair on a man's top lip

paint *(v)* to make a picture with colours

passage a narrow way in a building that goes to other rooms

plant *(n)* anything (e.g. flowers, trees) that is growing

poster a big piece of paper with words and pictures on it

pot a round 'box' to put things in

private   for one person or a small number of people only

record *(n)*   a round black thing that you put on a record-player
   to play music

rocks   very big pieces of stone

sad   not happy

spoil   to hurt or damage something so that it is useless or no
   good

tourist   a person on holiday

worry   to feel that something is wrong or will be wrong

Dead Man's Island

ACTIVITIES

Before Reading

1 The title of the story is *Dead Man's Island*. Can you guess the answers to these questions?

1 Where is the island?
   a) England   c) the USA
   b) Scotland   d) Australia
2 Is the dead man . . .
   a) a writer?   c) a businessman?
   b) a farmer?   d) a teacher?

2 Read the back cover of the book. Tick one box for each sentence.

	YES	NO	PERHAPS
1 Mr Ross has a secret.	☐	☐	☐
2 Mr Ross is unhappy.	☐	☐	☐
3 Mr Ross is young.	☐	☐	☐
4 Mr Ross is rich.	☐	☐	☐
5 Carol has a secret.	☐	☐	☐
6 Carol is unhappy.	☐	☐	☐
7 Carol is young.	☐	☐	☐
8 Carol is rich.	☐	☐	☐

Now read the story introduction on the first page of the book. Change some of your answers above if you want to.

3 Choose a possible ending for the story.

1 Mr Ross kills Carol.

2 Mr Ross and Carol get married.

3 Carol kills Mr Ross.

4 Mr Ross helps Carol to be happier.

5 Carol helps Mr Ross to be happier.

4 Before you read Chapters 1 and 2, can you guess the answers to these questions? These are the chapter titles:

Chapter 1 Coming to England
Chapter 2 The island

1 Who comes to England?

a) Carol and her mother

b) Mr Ross

c) Carol's mother and father

d) Mr Ross's wife

2 Who lives on the island?

a) Mr Ross

b) Mr Ross and 500 other people

c) Mr Ross and Mrs Ross

d) Mr Ross and a few people

While Reading

Read Chapter 1, then answer these questions.

1 Where did Carol live when she was younger?
2 Who was her favourite singer?
3 What happened to him?
4 How did Carol's father die?
5 How did Carol feel after her father's death?
6 Why did Carol have to leave the college?
7 What was Carol going to do in the autumn?
8 Why did Carol and her mother look in the newspapers?

Read Chapter 2 and complete these sentences about the people who live on the island.

1 _____ Duncan is the boatman.
2 Mrs Duncan is the _____.
3 Mr _____ is the gardener.
4 Mr Ross is a _____.
5 Greta Ross is his _____.
6 Mr Ross's _____ is in hospital.
7 Dan and Stella _____ work on the farm.
8 _____ is going to work on the farm too.

Read Chapter 3. Are these sentences true (T) or false (F)? Change the false sentences into true ones.

1 Carol's mother worked very hard.

2 Mr Ross owns the island.

3 The island had a lot of visitors.

4 Mr Ross took a photograph of Carol.

5 Carol didn't open the locked door.

Read Chapter 4, then answer these questions.

Who

1 . . . was hot and couldn't sleep?

2 . . . was in the locked room?

3 . . . hid the key in the plant pot?

4 . . . was working at her desk?

5 . . . went out in the boat?

Before you read Chapter 5, can you guess what is in the locked room? Choose Y (Yes) or N (No) each time.

1 a dead man Y/N

2 a lot of money Y/N

3 clothes Y/N

4 an animal Y/N

5 guitars Y/N

6 a piano Y/N

7 computers Y/N

8 photographs Y/N

9 drugs Y/N

After Reading

1 **Match these halves of sentences to make a summary of Jake Rosso's story in Chapter 5.**

1 When Jake Rosso was driving his car one night,
2 He hit a young girl
3 He didn't tell the police about the accident
4 So he put a guitar and some clothes in his car
5 When the police found the burned car,
6 After some months, Greta changed her name to Ross
7 Now Mr Ross lives very quietly
8 because he was afraid.
9 they thought Jake Rosso was dead.
10 he had an accident.
11 and she died.
12 and then he pushed the car over a cliff and burned it.
13 and bought the island with Jake Rosso's money.
14 but he can never forget the young girl who died.

2 **Put these words into two lists under the headings. Then tick the job that you prefer.**

| farmer | businessman/woman |

garden, telephone, secretary, sheep, cows, computer, chickens, desk, office, vegetables, fruit, letters

Saddletowne Library
Self Checkout
December,10 2018 14 45

39065137108856   12/31/2018
Dead man's island

Total   1 item(s)

You have 0 item(s) ready for pickup

Come visit your new Central Library!

Enjoy free tours, activities, and events.

Visit our website to find out what's on

calgarylibrary.ca/new-central-library

To check your card and renew items

go to www.calgarylibrary.ca

or call 403-262-2928

3 **Match the people with the sentences. Then use the sentences to write a short description of each person. Use pronouns (*he, she*) and linking words (*and, but, so*) where possible.**

Carol / Mrs Sanders / Mr Ross / Greta Ross
Example: *Carol is eighteen. <u>She</u> likes riding and gardening, and she* . . .

1 *Carol* is eighteen.
2 _____ has very long dark hair.
3 _____ is Carol's mother.
4 _____ was a famous pop star called Jake Rosso.
5 _____ is very beautiful.
6 _____ was married to a businessman.
7 _____ likes swimming and painting.
8 _____'s real name is James Duncan.
9 _____ is Tony Duncan's brother.
10 _____ isn't lonely on the island.
11 _____ works as a secretary.
12 *Carol* likes riding and gardening.
13 _____ has a moustache, short dark hair and glasses.
14 _____ owns the island, house and farm.
15 _____ never leaves the island.
16 _____ works very hard.
17 _____ wants to be a farmer.

4 Jake, Greta and Carol could choose to do different things in this story. Here are some of the things they could choose to do. Are they better (B) or worse (W) than what happens in the book? Explain why.

  1 After the car accident, Jake Rosso says:
    a) 'I'm going to tell the police.'
    b) 'I'm going to keep my money and go to live in South America.'
  2 After the accident, Greta Ross says to Jake:
    a) 'I'll keep your secret, but I'm going to leave you.'
    b) 'I'm going to tell the police.'
  3 After she goes inside the locked room, Carol says to Mr Ross:
    a) 'I'm going to tell the police.'
    b) 'I'll keep your secret but I want a lot of money.'

5 Do you agree (A) or disagree (D) with these sentences? Explain why.

  1 You must always tell someone when you do something wrong.
  2 You must always keep another person's secret.

6 Imagine that you are Carol. Use the words below to write a letter to a friend. You think there is something strange about Mr Ross. Explain why.

be / young and rich; not like / visitors; never leave / island, not like / photographs; have / locked room / house

Dear . . .
I've been here on the island for a week. It's very beautiful, and everyone is very friendly, but Mr Ross is really strange. He . . .

7 Jake Rosso has just come home after the accident. He is talking to Greta. Complete their conversation.

GRETA: Jake, what's happened?
JAKE: I _____
GRETA: Oh no! Did you tell the police?
JAKE: No _____
GRETA: What are you going to do?
JAKE: I _____
GRETA: How are you going to fake it?
JAKE: I _____
GRETA: Then what will we do? Where will we live?
JAKE: You _____
GRETA: What about your music?
JAKE: I _____

ABOUT THE AUTHOR

John Escott worked in business before becoming a writer. Since then he has written many books for readers of all ages, but enjoys writing crime and mystery thrillers most of all. He was born in Somerset, in the west of England, but now lives in Bournemouth on the south coast. When he is not working, he likes looking for long-forgotten books in small back-street bookshops, watching old Hollywood films on video, and walking for miles along empty beaches.

He has written or retold many stories for the Oxford Bookworms Library. His original stories include *Goodbye, Mr Hollywood* (at Stage 1) and *Agatha Christie, Woman of Mystery* (at Stage 2), which is the true story of the life of perhaps the most famous crime author in the world.

OXFORD BOOKWORMS LIBRARY

Classics • Crime & Mystery • Factfiles • Fantasy & Horror
Human Interest • Playscripts • Thriller & Adventure
True Stories • World Stories

The OXFORD BOOKWORMS LIBRARY provides enjoyable reading in English, with a wide range of classic and modern fiction, non-fiction, and plays. It includes original and adapted texts in seven carefully graded language stages, which take learners from beginner to advanced level. An overview is given on the next pages.

All Stage 1 titles are available as audio recordings, as well as over eighty other titles from Starter to Stage 6. All Starters and many titles at Stages 1 to 4 are specially recommended for younger learners. Every Bookworm is illustrated, and Starters and Factfiles have full-colour illustrations.

The OXFORD BOOKWORMS LIBRARY also offers extensive support. Each book contains an introduction to the story, notes about the author, a glossary, and activities. Additional resources include tests and worksheets, and answers for these and for the activities in the books. There is advice on running a class library, using audio recordings, and the many ways of using Oxford Bookworms in reading programmes. Resource materials are available on the website <www.oup.com/elt/gradedreaders>.

The *Oxford Bookworms Collection* is a series for advanced learners. It consists of volumes of short stories by well-known authors, both classic and modern. Texts are not abridged or adapted in any way, but carefully selected to be accessible to the advanced student.

You can find details and a full list of titles in the *Oxford Bookworms Library Catalogue* and *Oxford English Language Teaching Catalogues*, and on the website <www.oup.com/elt/gradedreaders>.

THE OXFORD BOOKWORMS LIBRARY
GRADING AND SAMPLE EXTRACTS

STARTER • 250 HEADWORDS

present simple – present continuous – imperative –
can/cannot, must – *going to* (future) – simple gerunds ...

Her phone is ringing – but where is it?

Sally gets out of bed and looks in her bag. No phone. She looks under the bed. No phone. Then she looks behind the door. There is her phone. Sally picks up her phone and answers it. *Sally's Phone*

STAGE 1 • 400 HEADWORDS

... past simple – coordination with *and, but, or* –
subordination with *before, after, when, because, so* ...

I knew him in Persia. He was a famous builder and I worked with him there. For a time I was his friend, but not for long. When he came to Paris, I came after him – I wanted to watch him. He was a very clever, very dangerous man. *The Phantom of the Opera*

STAGE 2 • 700 HEADWORDS

... present perfect – *will* (future) – *(don't) have to, must not, could* –
comparison of adjectives – simple *if* clauses – past continuous –
tag questions – *ask/tell* + infinitive ...

While I was writing these words in my diary, I decided what to do. I must try to escape. I shall try to get down the wall outside. The window is high above the ground, but I have to try. I shall take some of the gold with me – if I escape, perhaps it will be helpful later. *Dracula*

STAGE 3 • 1000 HEADWORDS

… should, may – present perfect continuous – *used to* – past perfect –
causative – relative clauses – indirect statements …

Of course, it was most important that no one should see
Colin, Mary, or Dickon entering the secret garden. So Colin
gave orders to the gardeners that they must all keep away
from that part of the garden in future. *The Secret Garden*

STAGE 4 • 1400 HEADWORDS

… past perfect continuous – passive (simple forms) –
would conditional clauses – indirect questions –
relatives with *where/when* – gerunds after prepositions/phrases …

I was glad. Now Hyde could not show his face to the world
again. If he did, every honest man in London would be proud
to report him to the police. *Dr Jekyll and Mr Hyde*

STAGE 5 • 1800 HEADWORDS

… future continuous – future perfect –
passive (modals, continuous forms) –
would have conditional clauses – modals + perfect infinitive …

If he had spoken Estella's name, I would have hit him. I was so
angry with him, and so depressed about my future, that I could
not eat the breakfast. Instead I went straight to the old house.
Great Expectations

STAGE 6 • 2500 HEADWORDS

… passive (infinitives, gerunds) – advanced modal meanings –
clauses of concession, condition

When I stepped up to the piano, I was confident. It was as if I
knew that the prodigy side of me really did exist. And when I
started to play, I was so caught up in how lovely I looked that
I didn't worry how I would sound. *The Joy Luck Club*

Death in the Freezer

TIM VICARY

Ellen Shore's family is an ordinary American family, and Ellen is six years old when her brother Al is born. Her parents are very pleased to have a son, but Ellen is not pleased, because now baby Al comes first.

And when they are adults, Al still comes first. He begins a rock band and makes records. Soon he is rich and famous – very rich, but he gives nothing to his sister Ellen. She has a difficult life, with three young kids and very little money. And she learns to hate her rich, famous, unkind brother ...

Love among the Haystacks

D. H. LAWRENCE

Retold by Jennifer Bassett

It is hay-making time on the Wookey farm. Two brothers are building the haystack, but thinking about other things - about young women, and love. There are angry words, and then a fight between the brothers. But the work goes on, visitors come and go, and the long hot summer day slowly turns to evening.

Then the sun goes down, covering the world with a carpet of darkness. From the hedges around the hayfield comes the rich, sweet smell of wild flowers, and the hay will make a fine, soft bed ...